101 Ar

MW01273286

Do in Sri Lanka

© 2018 101 Amazing Things

Introduction

So you're going to Sri Lanka huh? You are very very lucky indeed! You are sure in for a treat because Sri Lanka is a special place that offers tonnes to explore, whether you're obsessed with nature, you're a culture vulture, or you just fancy eating some yummy food.

This guide will take you on a journey across all the major tourist destinations, from the cities like Colombo and Galle, through to coastal towns like Arugam Bay and Mirissa, as well as the mountains, tea plantations, and places of historical importance.

In this guide, we'll be giving you the low down on:
- the very best things to shove in your pie hole, from comfort food like Sri Lankan chicken curry through to the best seafood restaurants to get a taste of the Indian ocean
- incredible festivals, whether you would like to party on the beach or discover Colombo's burgeoning arts scene
- the coolest historical and cultural sights that you simply cannot afford to miss like monasteries hidden away in

caves or museums that can teach you about the history of Buddhism in the country

- the most incredible outdoor adventures, whether you want to have a canyoning adventure on the Kelani river or you'd like to try deep sea fishing

- and tonnes more coolness besides!

Let's not waste any more time – here are the 101 amazing, spectacular, and cool things not to miss in Sri Lanka!

1. Visit an Iconic Place of Buddhist Worship

Most local people in Sri Lanka are Buddhists, and the most important place of worship for the Buddhist population in the whole country is Colombo's Gangaramaya Temple. Built in the 19th century, the architecture of the temple is very interesting, with a mix of Sri Lankan, Thai, Indian, and Chinese influences. As well as being a beautiful place, walking around the premises also offers spectacular views of the surrounding area.

(61 Sri Jinarathana Rd, Colombo 00200, http://gangaramaya.com)

2. Have a Typical Lunch of Fish Curry & Rice

If you want to experience the true Sri Lanka, you have to make the effort to eat like a local. This means going to local eateries, eating with your hands, and getting the chance to chat to locals who are taking their lunch breaks. By far the most common meal you'll find as a local lunch is fish curry and rise. That might sound basic, but the delight of the dish is in its simplicity. And because Sri Lanka is surrounded by water, you can be assured that the fish is totally fresh.

3. Enjoy Lazy Beach Days at Tangalla

Since Sri Lanka is completely surrounded by water, you have more than a few options for stellar beach breaks in the tropical sunshine, and one of the lesser visited beaches that you absolutely need to check out is called Tangalla. Some of the beach destinations in Sri Lanka are Party Central, but this is the place for you if you simply want to relax and enjoy the country at its idyllic best. The sand is golden, the water is warm, and it has a quaint, laid back feel.

4. Escape City Life in Viharamahadevi Park

As the capital city of Sri Lanka, Colombo is a place that is far more bustling than any other city in the country, and at times you may feel the need to escape the honking horns and enjoy a little peace of quiet inside the city. This is totally possible if you just head to Viharamahadevi Park. The park has recently undergone a massive renovation, and the results are fantastic. There are wall marked paths, a children's play area, pony rides, a lake, and lots of greenery to explore.

5. Join the Festivities of Kandy Esala Perahera

While most people choose to visit Sri Lanka in the winter months when the temperature is typically cooler, visiting in the summertime has its benefits too, not least because you'll have a chance to celebrate the Kandy Esala Perahera, which takes place in Kandy throughout July and

August. The historical procession is held each year as a way of paying homage to the Sacred Tooth Relic of Lord Buddha. The processions contain dressed up elephants and many local dances.

6. Discover Village Life at Ape Gama

If you are not so keen on walking the aisles of stuffy museums, we think that Ape Gama is the kind of museum that might just pull your arm and get you to see the museum experience in a completely different light. Instead of housing artefacts in lass cabinets, Ape Gama is a museum that actually attempts to recreate village life across Sri Lanka. You'll find the village houses of people like weavers, and blacksmiths, the objects they would use day-to-day, and some very lovely gardens.

(Sri Jayawardenepura Kotte)

7. Take a Jeep Safari Tour of Yala National Park

Sri Lanka is one of the best places to have a jeep safari adventure in the whole world, and there are a couple of parks where you can see wild animals in their natural habitat. Yala National Park is one of these with safari experiences every day of the week. Some of the animals that you can expect to see up close are the Sri Lankan elephant, water buffalos, leopards, sloth bears, and many birds.

8. Indulge a History Buff at the National Museum of Colombo

If you are a museum lover, there isn't the hugest selection of museums in this country, but there's definitely a handful that are worth exploring in Sri Lanka, and the National Museum of Colombo is most definitely the jewel in the crown of the country's museum scene. The museum opened all the way back in 1877, and its collection has grown exponentially since then. Inside you'll find special items such as palm leaves inscribed in Sinhala, and the thrones of Kandyan monarchs.

(Sir Marcus Fernando Mawatha, Colombo 00700)

9. Be Charmed by the Stick No Bills Poster Gallery

Galle is a place that is absolutely bursting full of charm, and one of the most charming places that will appeal hugely to artsy types is the No Bills Poster Gallery. Located in a stunning Dutch colonial era townhouse, this gallery is dedicated to showcasing rare travel and film posters from the 19th and 20th centuries. They also sell their own high quality lithograph posters and postcards, which are great gifts or souvenirs.

10. Climb Adam's Peak Through the Night

One of the most iconic hikes and lookout points in Sri Lanka is Adam's Peak, which is located a little way outside of Kandy. The mountain is also known as Sri Pada, and has a 2243 metre elevation. The hike is typically started in the middle of the night so that you can reach the peak for sunrise. This is a scared place for people of many religions. Buddhists believe it contains a footprint mark from Buddha, Hindus believe it belongs to Shiva, and Christians and Muslims believe it was Adam's first step outside the garden of Eden.

11. Party on the Sand for Hikkaduwa Beach Festival

Sri Lanka is a country with some of the most beautiful beaches in Asia, and a unique way to enjoy these beaches is to party hard on the beach at a beach festival. If that sounds like a good time to you then you should know about the annual Hikkaduwa Beach Festival, which is hosted in either July or August each year. Whether you are into EDM, jazz music, or cultural performances, there is something for everyone at this welcoming festival on the coast.

12. Eat Delicious Ice Cream at Dairy King in Galle

No matter what time of year you visit Galle, the weather is going to be hot, and with limited AC around the city, you'll need to find more inventive ways to cool down. Well, what better way could there be than chowing down on some ice cream straight from the freezer? Our favourite ice cream haunt in Galle is called Dairy King, which sounds like a chain but it's actually a family run affair. The passionfruit flavour is incredible.

(69 Church St, Galle 80000)

13. Visit a Buddhist Temple Steeped in History

The Kelaniya temple is a temple located just 7 miles outside of Colombo, and it's a place that's extremely important for local Buddhists. It is believed that the temple was hallowed during the final visit of the Lord Buddha to Sri Lanka, which would date the history of the temple to 500BC. This temple is famous for its image of the reclining Buddha, and for paintings by a native artist that depict events from the Buddha's life.

14. Watch a Cricket Match at R Premadasa Stadium

To say that cricket is a big deal in Sri Lanka would be an understatement, and the best way to get your head around this national obsession is to check out a cricket match for yourself. There are numerous cricket stadiums dotted around the country, and one of the best of these is the R Premadesa Stadium, which you can find in Colombo. The stadium can fit more than 35,000 people, so when it's busy the atmosphere is electric.

(Khettarama Temple Rd, Colombo 01000)

15. Relax With an Ayurvedic Spa Experience

Going on holiday is a time when you can relax, recuperate, and hopefully feel totally refreshed by the time you make it back to your home country. In Sri Lanka, one of the very best ways of restoring your body back to its full glory is to indulge in an Ayurvedic treatment. Ayurveda is an ancient form of medicine that involves diet change, steam baths, massages, and oil treatments. There are plenty of Ayurvedic spas all over the country, so whether you just want to release some tension in your shoulders, or you want a full body VAT, you'll find a treatment to suit you.

16. Have a Snorkelling Adventure Off Pigeon Island

Since Sri Lanka is totally surrounded by water, there are plenty of places where water babies can have an adventure.

And actually, there is a world of marine life lurking in the surrounding oceans that are just waiting to be discovered. One of the most rewarding ways of doing this is by heading to Pigeon Island and snorkelling in the waters there. There are plenty of tour companies that provide this experience, and in the water you'll find the blacktip reef shark, many types of turtles, hundred of species of coral, and lots of colourful tropical fish.

17. Cool Down With a King Coconut From the Street

Everyone has tried coconuts, but what about the King Coconut? Well, as the name would suggest, this is like a coconut, but better! And as the fruit is indigenous to Sri Lanka, you need to chow down on them while you are on holiday on this beautiful island. Instead of having a green shell, the King Coconut has an outer orange skin, it is larger, and it has electrolyte levels close to human plasma. Beyond this, it's absolutely delicious, and purchasing some of this fruit from a street vendor is an awesome way to cool down in the tropical heat.

18. Eat Street Food at Galle Face in Colombo

If you find yourself in Colombo, and you'd prefer to have a cheap and cheerful meal instead of a sit down dinner in a restaurant, there are plenty of street food options, and one of the best places to find lots of different street food vendors is at Galle Face in the city. At around 5pm, many vendors start to wheel out their carts. You can buy deep fried samosas, grilled chicken, kottu, fresh fruits, wood apple juice, and lots more besides.

19. Go Whale Watching at Uppuveli Beach

Uppuveli is a lovely little local beach on the east coast that only plays host to a few hundred locals. This makes it the ideal place to get away from it all, but if you are in need of more adventure than that, you should also be aware that the waters off of this part of the coast are the perfect place for dolphin and whale watching. There's a big population of blue whales here, which are the largest animals to have ever lived.

20. Catch the Sunset at Flag Rock in Galle

Galle is a very picturesque small city, but if you would like to know the ultimate place for a mesmerising view in Galle, we recommend making your way to Flag Rock. You can find flag rock at the southern end of the fort, and it's an ideal place to look out over the ocean when the sunset strikes. This is also a nice place to grab some street snacks, and we can't recommend the fresh papaya sprinkled with chilli highly enough.

21. Hike to the Peak of Ella Rock

For adventurers, the small town of Ella in the Central Highlands is a must visit place. One of the hikes that is really quite challenging but doesn't take too much time is the hike to Ella's Rock. It can be helpful to hire a guide to show you the way to the peak, and it should take about 3 hours to get to the top. We recommend setting off early to beat the strong sun. Needless to say, at the top you'll have a view of the surrounding mountains and tea plantations that's well worth the slog.

22. Learn Something New at the National Museum of Galle

Although Galle is a small city, it has some rather impressive museums for a place of its size, and the National Museum of Galle might be the best of the lot. The museum is located in the oldest remaining Dutch building in the Galle Fort, and it dates way back to 1656. Inside, you can find objects from the Dutch, Portuguese, and British periods of rule. You can see things like furniture, lacework, weaponry, and mask carvings.

(Church St, Galle 80000)

23. Visit the Sacred Bodhi Tree Temple

Buddhism is the official religion of Sri Lanka, and one of the most important Buddhist relics to be found in the country is the Jaya Sri Maha Bodhi, a sacred Bodhi or fig tree. It was under the branches of this tree that the Lord Buddha was believed to have attained Enlightenment. As such, it is very common for Buddhists in Sri Lanka, and indeed around the world, to visit this tree as a pilgrimage, and give their offerings.

(http://srimahabodhi.org)

24. Discover the Remains of Ritigala

Ritigala is a place in central Sri Lanka that combines the very best of nature and culture. Here you can find a mountain within a nature reserve, and the ruins of an ancient Buddhist monastery. It is home to 70 rock caves that are believed to have been inhabited since the 1st century BC, and the rock inscriptions found inside the caves show that this became a living space for hermit monks. The ruins of the monastery people see today was originally built in the 9th century.

25. Learn About Tea in Sri Lanka at the Ceylon Tea Museum

On your trip to Sri Lanka it won't be long before you realise just how important tea is to this nation, both historically and today. One of the best places to get a real sense of how tea has contributed to Sri Lanka economically, culturally, and gastronomically is by visiting the Ceylon Tea Museum, just outside of Kandy. The museum occupies the 1925 vintage Hantane Tea Factory, and inside you'll find exhibits on the tea pioneers, and lots of tea related paraphernalia.

(Hantana Rd, www.ceylonteamuseum.com)

26. Visit the Breath Taking Lankatilaka Temple

If you are a history buff, you shouldn't miss the opportunity to visit the Lankatilaka Tample, which is a 14th century Buddhist temple, built in the Kandy region, and it is considered to be the finest example of architecture from the Gampola era. The temple was originally created as a grand four storied mansion, but these days you can only see three stories. Rock inscriptions can be found inside the temple in Tamil and Sinhala.

27. Fill Your Tummy at the Sri Lankan Food Festival

There is so much to eat in Sri Lanka that the choice can be somewhat overwhelming, but one place where you can try lots of different types of Sri Lankan food, snacks, and drinks is at the annual Sri Lankan Food Festival, which is hosted in Colombo in October each year. You can expect to try lots of traditional dishes, signature plates from some of the most celebrated restaurants in town, and cooking demonstrations as well.

28. Go Birdwatching in Kalametiya Sanctuary

One of the things that tourists go to Sri Lanka specially for is the safari experience. But mammals on the ground are not the only animals to be found in the country, and if you look to the skies you will also see some incredible bird life. One of the best spots in Sri Lanka for birdwatching has to be the Kalametiya Sanctuary, which you can find on the south coast. You'll find 230 bird species living in the mangroves and beach area.

(Hambantota Road, Nonagama)

29. Wave a Rainbow Flag at Colombo Pride

Being LGBT in Sri Lanka is a challenge to say the least. Same sex sexual activity is illegal in the country, and there is absolutely no recognition of same sex relationships. This means that Colombo Pride is an event unlike other Pride events you might have attended where you live. This is a subsection of the local community that struggles for visibility, and this event gives the local LGBT population that opportunity. It takes place each year in early June, so if you are there do lend your support and enjoy the parties and parades.

(http://equal-ground.org)

30. Tour the Newburgh Green Tea Factory in Ella

Sri Lanka is a country that is famous for its tea production, but this is a nation that drinks black tea almost exclusively. If you'd like to understand different types of tea production in the country, a visit to the Newburgh Green Tea Factory in Ella could be a great idea. You'll learn how green tea is produced from beginning to end, and, of course, you'll get to sip on some of the good stuff.

31. Fill Your Stomach With Young Jackfruit Curry

Some people think that Sri Lanka must just be like south Indian food. Well, there is definitely some overlap, but with that said, it's totally possible to find culinary delights that are native to Sri Lanka and that you can only find in the country. Young jackfruit curry is one such dish. As you can imagine, the fruit in the curry provides a sweet element, which when combined with the numerous spices and coconut milk is something really special.

32. Tour the Ancient Ruins of Polonnaruwa

If you have any interest in history, you are certainly going to the right place, because there are many ancient ruins to be explored all over the country. The city of Polonnaruwa was the second capital of Ceylon, from the end of the 10th century. It is now one of the best planned archaeological relic sites in the whole country, and walking around these ruins (amongst the monkeys who live there) is sure to take you back in time.

(http://whc.unesco.org/en/list/201)

33. Get Back to Nature in Hakgala Gardens

When you're in Sri Lanka, you won't have too many problems getting back to nature as there is an immense amount of greenery dotted around. But one of the best spots to immerse yourself in everything green is at Hakgala Gardens in Nuwara Eliya. In fact, this is one of only five botanical gardens in the country. Inside, you'll find beautiful orchid species, rose species, and many other plants and flowers.

(Peradeniya-Badulla-Chenkaladi Highway, Hakgala)

34. Chow Down on Sri Lankan Chicken Curry

Chicken curry is something that you have probably eaten before. There are varieties of chicken curry in places as far reaching as Japan, China, and Rajasthan, and each one is slightly unique in its flavour profile. The Sri Lankan chicken curry is no exception. Two of the key ingredients in this version are tamarind and coconut milk. The tamarind provides sourness and depth of the flavour, while the coconut milk adds sweetness and creaminess.

35. Visit the Beautiful Ravana Falls

There is nothing quite as appealing as a gushing waterfall on a hot day, and there are plenty of waterfalls to enjoy in Sri Lanka. One of the most special of these is the Ravana Falls, and it's one of the widest falls in the country. Of course, it's best to visit the falls in the monsoon season when the water is gushing at its most powerful but there is water there at any time of year. Excavations in the cave by the falls reveal human life dating back to 25,000 years ago.

36. Cycle Along the Canals of Negombo

If you are the kind of person who loves nothing more than to explore a new area while sitting on a push bike, you'll need to know the best places in Sri Lanka that you can explore. Forget the mountains, and head to the coastal town of Negombo if you would like to have a manageable cycling experience. In Negombo, there is a network of canals that were built by the Dutch, and the pathways alongside the canals offer flat cycling terrain.

37. Try Jet Ski Riding in Bentota

As an island surrounded by water, Sri Lanka is the perfect place to really explore the ocean, and enjoy some daring watersports. One of the most thrilling of all these sports has to be jet skiing. If you are something of a daredevil and you like the idea of being pulled across the open waters by a speed boat zooming in front of you, why not try it out? Bentota is a great spot for trying this out.

38. Buy a Carved Mask From Ambalangoda

Ambalangoda is an overlooked beach town because it's very much a working coastal town that is not built for tourists, but in our opinion that is what is so cool about it. And what's extra special about this town is that is has an awesome culture of producing traditional crafts, and the most famous of all these crafts in Sri Lanka would have to be carved wooden masks. These devil masks are supposed to drive out evil spirits that cause illness.

39. Have a Sailing Adventure Off the Coast of Negombo

If you are the kind of person who loves being in the water, you have chosen well by visiting the island of Sri Lanka. Many of the coastal towns offer up activities on the water, and for a spot of sailing, Negombo, which is only one hour away from Colombo, is the ideal place. The water and wind conditions are perfect for taking to the water, and it's possible to book sailing tours from as little as an hour on the seas.

40. Pay a Visit to the Oldest Hindu Temple in Colombo

Although there is a Buddhist majority in Colombo, you can actually find places of worship from many religions, and one of the most important centres for Hinduism in the capital city is a temple called Sri Kailawasanathar Swami Devasthanam. This is the oldest Hindu temple in the whole city, and this makes it an important and sacred place for the local Hindu population. The carvings on the exterior of the building are incredibly intricate.

41. Get Artsy at the Colombo Art Biennale

For artsy types, Sri Lanka might not seem like the obvious holiday destination. It's true that the country doesn't have huge art galleries like some other places in the world, but if you are into art, be sure to visit in December so that your trip coincides with the Colombo Art Biennale. This art festival is dedicated to showcasing the world of local Sri Lankan artists, so it's an incredible way of getting your teeth stuck into the local creative scene.

(http://colomboartbiennale.com)

42. Party on the Beach in Unawatuna

If you are a party person who loves to dance through the night, you'll have to do a bit of searching in Sri Lanka, because this is more of a place to get back to nature, and enjoy cultural attractions. With that said, party lovers can always find a party, and the place to be for drinking, dancing, and music is Unawatuna, a little beach outside of Galle that's very popular with backpackers. You can party hard at all of the beach bars until the sun comes up.

43. Visit the Ancient Rock Fortress of Sigiriya

In a country full of dramatic landscapes, Sigiriya might just be the most dramatic, and perhaps most iconic, sight of them all. You can find the ruins of the ancient capital called Sigiriya at the top of a granite peak with almost vertical slopes. It was thought to be the epicentre of the Kassapa Kingdom, and so it's a must visit for all history buffs. You can only ascend to the top via winding staircases, and the surrounding landscape includes lily pad covered moats, water gardens, and shrines.

44. Try the Sri Lankan Cheeseburger, Kottu

All the new food you will try in Sri Lanka will be spectacular, but there are times when all you want to eat is a cheeseburger, right? Well, fortunately for you, there is a Sri Lankan street food dish which could actually be interpreted as the country's version of a cheeseburger, and this is kottu. Instead of a bun, you get a roti, and the roti, meat, and cheese is all shredded up on one plate. This is comfort food at its best.

45. Get to Grips With Market Culture in Pettah Market

To get to know a place, it's a great idea to explore it from within one of its markets, and Colombo has a lively market culture that is just waiting to be explored. Now, this is not a market that is designed for tourists, which is a double edged sword. It means that you get the true local experience, but you won't experience any niceties. The market is hectic and you'll have to bargain hard, but you might just emerge with some special to take home.

46. Spend an Afternoon at the National Museum of Natural History

Most people who visit Sri Lanka are aware that the country holds many impressive natural wonders, but it's impossible to step into a time machine and understand how Sri Lanka's natural world has developed over time. But the next best thing is visiting the National Museum of Natural History in Colombo. The museum contains fossils of many species that are endemic to Sri Lanka, dating all the way back to Jurassic period.

(Sir Marcus Fernando Mawatha, Colombo 00700)

47. Find Something Special in Olanda Antiques in Galle

Galle is a very cute little city, and it's an awesome place to do a spot of shopping before you head back to your home country. One of the best nooks for shopping in the city is at Olanda Antiques, an antiques shop that is located in a Dutch colonial house. Unfortunately, you probably won't be able to fit many of their vintage furniture items into your luggage, but for small pieces like jewellery, it's a wonderful place to find something special.

(http://olandafurniture.com/)

48. Party on the Beach at ATMAN Festival

If you can't get enough of outdoor music festivals, Sri Lanka might not be the first country on your festival hitlist, but there are some parties here that are well worth exploring, including the relatively new ATMAN Festival. The music festival takes place in January each year at the ever popular Arugam Bay. If the sound of dancing to psychedelic tunes on the beach while making new friends sounds good to you, ATMAN could be the festival for you.

(www.atman-festival.com)

49. Enjoy a Horse Ride Around Gregory Lake

There is a huge amount to explore around Sri Lanka, but sometimes all you want is a day of relaxation and taking it easy. When that moment strikes, it's a very good idea to head to Gregory Lake, which you can find in the Nuwara Eliya area of the country. There are many ways to enjoy this picturesque landscapes: you can embark on long hikes, you can take boat trips, but our favourite thing is to take horse rides around, and it's something that kids love too.

50. Learn About Buddhism at the International Buddhist Museum

Sri Lanka is officially a Buddhist country, and while going to the many temples dotted around the country can be a great way of absorbing the local Buddhist culture, we also think that a trip to the International Buddhist Museum in Kandy would be a very good idea. This is a place to learn about Buddhism way beyond Sri Lanka, with contributions from places like China, India, Thailand, Korea, and Bhutan.

(Temple of the Tooth, Sri Dalada Veediya, Kandy, http://ibm.sridaladamaligawa.lk)

51. Explore a Cave Monastery in Dambulla

The Dambulla Cave Temple has to be one of the most unique temples that we have ever had the pleasure of visiting. Quite unbelievably, this has been a sacred pilgrimage site for 22 centuries now, and with five sanctuaries, it is the largest and best preserved cave complex to be found anywhere in the country. Inside, you will find 153 Buddha statues, and murals that cover an area of 2100 square metres.

52. Take a Hot Shower at the Kanniya Hot Springs

The Kanniya hot springs are probably not like any hot springs that you have ever encountered before. These are actually a series of wells in the ground that are about 3-4 feet deep. This means that you can't take a dip, but you can put in a bucket and give yourself a warm shower with the water. What makes the springs special is that the springs are connected to King Ravana who was said to have created them in 5000 BC.

53. Pick Your Own Strawberries in Nuwara Eliya

Strawberries are one of those food that absolutely everyone loves. You would probably associate strawberries with places that have a cooler climate, but that's exactly what you can experience in the mountains of the country, so you can actually find some strawberry farms dotted around Sri Lanka. Adma Agro in Nuwara Eliya is one of the most beloved of these. This is because visitors are actually given the opportunity to pick their own strawberries and devour them.

(Peradeniya-Badulla-Chenkaladi Highway, Nuwara Eliya)

54. Hike in Horton Plains National Park

If your idea of the perfect getaway is strapping on your hiking boots and immersing yourself in the tranquillity that Mother Nature has to offer, you need to know about Horton Plains National Park, which can be found in the Central Highlands. The plains consist of huge expanses of grassland, think forest, misty lakes, gushing waterfalls, and rocky outcrops. Get there in the early morning before the clouds roll in.

55. Take a Pilgrimage to Nainativu Island

The northern part of Sri Lanka is severely neglected by tourists, and we think that's all the more reason that you should visit. A very special island off the north coast is called Nainativu. This island is particularly important for local Buddhists, because it is said that the Buddha stopped on this island to resolve a conflict between the king and his son-in-law. The Nagadeepa Vihare Shrine is decorated with beautiful art, statues of animals, and is painted in silver unlike most Buddhist shrines.

56. Catch a Movie at the Galle Film Festival

When you are travelling, it's awesome to take in all the new sights and sounds and smells of the place, but this can be exhausting, and sometimes all you'll want to do is kick back with a good movie. Well, what better way of doing that in Sri Lanka than catching a few flicks at the Galle Film Festival? This film festival takes place over the end of October and beginning of November, when you can catch a selection of fringe films from South Asia and beyond.

(www.gallefilmfestival.com)

57. Join in With the Vesak Poya Celebrations

Since Sri Lanka is a Buddhist country, it can be a very good idea to join in with some of the Buddhist celebrations throughout the year, of which there are many. One of the most important and fun festivals is called Vesak Poya, and it celebrates the birth, the Enlightenment, and the death of the Buddha. It takes place in May, and it's otherwise known as the Celebration of Lights, so you can expect enchanting fireworks displays wherever you are in the country.

58. Tuck Into Yummy Ice Cream at AVM Cream House

When you want to cool down in the most delicious way possible, ice cream is always the answer, and that's why we can't recommend the AVM Cream House if Weligama highly enough. The fruit flavours are genuinely made from local fruits, so whether you go for papaya, mango, or king coconut, you are sure to get an authentic taste of the tropics. They will even contribute to your Vitamin C intake for the day!

59. Learn to Surf at Arugam Bay

As Sri Lanka is totally surrounded by water, you have the opportunity to check out many of the cool water activities of the lazy beach towns. Whether you are a seasoned surfer or you want to ride the waves of the ocean for the very first time, Arugam Bay is the place to be. There are plenty of surf schools here that can give you lessons, and where you can rent all the kit that you need - so why not give it a try?

60. Enjoy Live Music at the Music Matters Festival

If you love nothing more than jamming to the sounds of live music, you should know about the annual Music Matters Festival, which is hosted in capital city Colombo in August each year. Over the years, Music Matters has established itself as one of the must-visit events on the Colombo art calendar. This contemporary music event exposes visitors to music that is beyond the mainstream.

(www.musicmatterssrilanka.com/festival.php)

61. Tuck Into Gotukola Sambol

Sri Lankan food is totally delicious, but at times it can be difficult to find dishes with a lot of green vegetables. But there is one delicious plate that we can recommend for when you are in need of a dose of Vitamin C. Gotukula is the word for Asian pennywort, a leafy green vegetable that is very common over Asia, and that's the main ingredient of this dish. The greens are sliced thinly, and cooked with grated coconut, red onions, and a variety of spices.

62. Tour the Four Devales of Kandy

Sri Lanka is a deeply religious country, and one of the most important places for Buddhists is Kandy, where you can find the four devales of Kandy. Popular belief would have it that Kandy is protected by four gods, and each of these has its own special temple, or devale, in the centre of the city. It is possible to visit all four within an afternoon and really immerse yourself in the religious culture of the city.

63. Be Wowed by the Wolvendall Church in Colombo

The Dutch controlled much of Sri Lanka, or Ceylon as it was called historically, in the 17th and 18th centuries, and this means that you can see a lot of Dutch influence in buildings dotted around various cities. In Colombo, one of the most famous of these Dutch buildings is the Wolvendall Church, a church that was completed in 1757. The church was created in the Doric style of the period, in the form of a Greek cross.

(Wolfendhal Ln, Colombo 01300, www.wolvendaal.org/churches-monuments/wolvendaal-church-colombo)

64. Stroll Through the Kandy Garrison Cemetery

Okay, so visiting a cemetery on your travels to Sri Lanka might seem like a morbid thing to do, but a trip to the Kandy Garrison Cemetery can give you a great understanding of a certain part of the local history. This cemetery dates back to colonial times, and contains the graves of 195 British people. What's particularly striking as you wander around is the age of the dead, and how they died. Many died before 40, and died of things like jungle fever and sunstroke.

65. Indulge a Sweet Tooth With Pittu Funnel Cakes

When it comes to gastronomy in Sri Lanka, it's the savoury curries that steal all of the focus, but if you do have a sweet tooth, there is no reason to feel left out because there are also plenty of traditional sweets that you can enjoy on your trip to Sri Lanka. Pittu funnel cakes might just be our favourite of these treats. These cakes are made from flour and freshly ground coconut, but instead of being baked they are steamed, and then served alongside sweetened coconut milk.

66. Buy Beautiful Lacework at Shoba Display Gallery

Before you depart from Sri Lanka, you are bound to want to find some special souvenirs to take home with you. Trust us when we tell you to ditch the tacky souvenir shops and head for Shoba Display Gallery in Galle instead. Absolutely everything on display is created by a women's cooperative group and is created by hand and with loving care, with a specialism in lacework. There is also a café on site, and the opportunity to join in with one of the craft classes.

(Pedlar St, Galle 80000, www.shobafashion.org)

67. Spend Lazy Days on Perfect Mirissa Beach

Ask any traveller or indeed local person to recommend their favourite beach in Sri Lanka, and you are likely to be on the receiving end of a different answer every time. This is a testament to the quality of the beaches of Sri Lanka, but if pushed for our number one beach recommendation, we thank that picturesque Mirissa might just clinch it. As well as lazy beach days, this is also a popular spot for whale watching.

68. Get Spicy at the World Spice Food Festival

Sri Lanka is a country that is famous for the incredible spices that it grows in spice plantations, and that it uses in its various flavourful dishes. If you can't get enough spice in your life, the World Spice Food Festival in Colombo is a place where you can enjoy all the beauty of Sri Lankan spices. The festival will feature many cooking competitions, and, of course, plenty of food stalls so that you can fill your stomach.

69. Be Stunned by the Dutch Reformed Church in Galle

There is a mix of religions present in Sri Lanka, so don't be surprised to see beautiful churches as you walk around the country's streets. One of the most historically important churches in Sri Lanka is the Dutch Reformed Church of Galle. The present building dates back to the mid 18th century, and the organ from 1760 still sits within the church. This is a lovely place to pause and take some shade.

(Church Street, Galle)

70. Go Boating With Dolphins in Kalpitiya

The northwest of the country is somewhere that is almost altogether neglected by tourists, so if you want to get away from intense tourist crowds, the small fishing town of Kalpitiya might just be a good spot for you. There is hardly anything to do here, and that's part of the appeal. But if you want to have an adventure, it's possible to see schools of literally hundreds of dolphins offshore in the rough waters here.

71. Meditate at Nilambe Buddhist Meditation Centre

Meditation is one of the activities of practicing Buddhists, and as Sri Lanka is a Buddhist country, there are spots here and there where visitors are welcome to try out meditation as well. The Nilambe Buddhist Meditation Centre is probably the best known of these places. You don't need to have had any specific meditation experience to enroll – just an open mind. There are retreats of various lengths,

(http://nilambe.net)

72. Cool Down With Refreshing Wood Apple Juice

One of the best things about going to a foreign country for the first time is having the opportunity to try foods that you have never tried before, and something that might be new to you is the wood apple. Now, a wood apple doesn't resemble a conventional apple in the slightest. It actually looks like a mouldy coconut, and it has its own distinct smell of blue cheese and raisins. We know that doesn't sound so appealing, but when it gets blended up into a juice, it suddenly transforms and becomes a refreshing delight.

73. Visit the Ancient Holy Site of Mihintale

If you want to get off the beaten track in Sri Lanka and experience a quiet but very special place, we think that

Mihintale could be a place that's right up your alley. The reason why it's so special is because Mihintale is revered as the birthplace of Buddhism in Sri Lanka, with its origins in the 4th century BC. These days, you can still walk amongst the many beautiful shrines, stupas, and monk's caves that exist here.

74. Tuck Into Fresh Seafood at Elita Restaurant in Galle

Since Sri Lanka is an island nation surrounded by water, you can expect to enjoy some delicious seafood in the country's coastal locations. One of our top picks is Elita restaurant in Galle. There are tables out front that overlook the sea, and when you combine this with a whole crab curry, you can't expect lunchtimes to get much more wonderful.

(34 Middle St, Galle 80000)

75. Tour the Pedro Tea Factory

The hills of Sri Lanka are the ideal place for growing tea, and so it's here that you can tour many of the cute tea factories. We are particularly enamoured by the Pedro Tea Factory in Nuwara Eliya. This tea factory originally opened all the way back in 1885, so it's also a slice of local history. At the factory, you'll be shown how tea is grown, manufactured, packed, and then shipped to all corners of the world.

76. Watch Snake Charmers on the Streets of Colombo

Snake charmers are something very much associated with this part of Asia, and you can easily see one during your time in Colombo. To say exactly where is a little bit tricky because the snake charmers move around from place to place, but you can probably get lucky at one of the exits of Viharamahadevi Park. Be sure to give the charmer a good tip if you are impressed by this magic street show.

77. Stroll the Fort Walls of Galle at Dusk

Galle Fort has been described by UNESCO as one of the best examples of a European fortified city in South Asia. And although the fort walls are more than 430 years old, it is still possible to walk along the walls and explore the city in this charming way. We think that dusk is a particularly great time to walk the walls because you'll avoid the tourist crowds and you'll also escape the intense heat that descends upon the city later in the day.

78. Celebrate Sri Lanka Art at Kala Pola

When you think of nations around the world that are famous for their artistic contributions, Sri Lanka might not be the first place that springs into your mind, but this is not to say that there is no arts culture to be found here. One of the best places to feel the creative pulse of Sri Lanka, is at Kala Pola, an open art fair, which takes place in Colombo every January. This is a great place to find something really special from local artists to take home with you.

79. Stay on a Tea Plantation in Madulkelle

Something that Sri Lanka is very famous for is its tea plantations in the highlands. You are likely to visit a couple of these on your stay in the country, but how much cooler would it be if you could really absorb the Sri Lankan tea experience by staying on one of the plantations? Well, it turns out that you can at Madulkelle Tea and Eco Lodge. Walk the tea fields by the day, and then come back to enjoy decadent afternoon tea, and relax in your own lodge.

(Madolkele - Habaragala Rd, www.madulkelle.com)

80. Stroll the Royal Botanical Gardens of Peradeniya

Although Sri Lanka is a very rich country in terms of its flora, there aren't too many botanical gardens to be found.

One of the exceptions is the Royal Botanical Gardens of Peradeniya, which were once reserved exclusively for Kandyan royalty, but now anyone is welcome to stroll the 60 acres of the gardens. Highlights include a giant Javan fig tree and an avenue of royal palms.

(Peradeniya Rd, Kandy)

81. Climb Single Tree Hill for a Beautiful View

If you're looking for a spot for a brisk hike, there are endless paths you can take in Sri Lanka, and a good place to get started is among the hills of Nuwara Eliya. Not only is climbing to the peak of Single Tree Hill some great exercise, but it's also the place to enjoy the very best vistas of Nuwara Eliya. It takes about 90 minutes to get to the top, but the climb is very doable. Just make sure that you do it in the early morning before the fierce Sri Lankan sun rears its head.

82. Dance, Dance, Dance at Sunset Music Festival

Sri Lanka may not have a reputation as one of the countries around the world best known for parties and all-night DJ sets, but Sri Lanka becomes a dance lovers paradise in December every year when the Sunset Music Festival is hosted in Colombo. This festival attracts some of the best loved DJ talent to be found anywhere in the world, and previous DJ sets have come courtesy of the likes of David Guetta and Tiesto.

(www.smf.lk)

83. Be Impressed by the Royal Palace of Kandy

When in Kandy, history buffs should not miss the opportunity to visit the remains of the Royal Palace of Kandy. The first palace on this site was built in the 14th century, but it has long been destroyed, and the remains of the place that you can see today belong to the 18th century, and the last residence of the Kandyan Kingdom. Even today, you get a sense of the grandeur of the place.

84. Hit a Few Balls at the Victoria Golf Course

For some people, a perfect getaway is trying new foods, for others it's strolling ancient ruins, and then some people love nothing more than the simple pleasure of hitting a few golf balls. If you're a passionate golf player, there are some wonderful courses to explore around Sri Lanka, and one of the most acclaimed of these is Victoria Golf Course in the Kandy district. Although this is a pretty course, it will make even seasoned golfers work hard!

(https://golfsrilanka.com)

85. Get to Grips With Local Handicrafts at the Matale Heritage Centre

Matale is a place that too often gets left out on Sri Lanka tourist itineraries, but it's a great place to really get to grips with traditional Sri Lanka as it's a town with many beautiful crafts that are local to the area. The best place to explore these is at the Matale Heritage Centre. This centre for crafts produces incredible batik work, embroidery, carpentry, and brasswork. It's one of the best places in the country for souvenir shopping, in our opinion.

86. Take in the Vistas of Kandy View Point

Once you get into the mountains of Sri Lanka, you will be surrounded by the most epic views, and one viewpoint that you shouldn't miss is the Kandy View Point. It is only located 1 kilometre away from the centre of Kandy, so it's very easy to access. You can either walk upwards (be warned that it's a steep climb) or take a three wheeler, and from there, you can see all of Kandy, including the lake.

87. Trek Through the Sinharaja Rainforest

For a small country, Sri Lanka certainly does have an impressive breadth of landscapes, but the Sinharaja Forest Reserve in the southwest of the country is the only place where you can find tropical rainforest. Be sure to hire one of the park guides to take you on a trek through this unique part of Sri Lanka. Inside the forest lives sambar, leopards, rusted spotty cats, western giant squirrels, wild boar, barking deer, and more.

88. Have a Morning of Learning at the National Maritime Museum

As a nation surrounded by sea, the maritime history of Sri Lanka is of great importance in the country, and the best place to learn all about it is at the National Maritime Museum in Galle. Located inside the most incredible building, a warehouse that dates back to 1671, this museum contains an awesome collection of boat models, seafaring maps, and artefacts salvaged from shipwrecks to give a full picture of the country's maritime history.

(Queens St, Galle 80000)

89. Eat a Yummy Plate of Beetroot Curry

With chicken and fish abounding in many Sri Lankan dishes, vegetarian visitors to the country might be wondering about some of the local dishes they can consume. One of the most original Sri Lanka dishes, and one of the tastiest too, is beetroot curry . The beetroot is cooked in coconut milk and spices, making this sweet and spicy all at once. We think it makes a wonderful light alternative to standard curries on those hot Lanka days.

90. Celebrate the Independence Day of Sri Lanka

One of the biggest non-religious celebration days in Sri Lanka has to be Independence Day, which lands on February 4th, and you guessed it, celebrates the nation's independence from the British in the 1940s. You can find celebrations all over the country, but the capital city is an especially great place to be at this time of year. You can expect military parades, dancing in the streets, music concerts, flags and banners waving in the air, and people eating food and drink on the street.

91. Enjoy a Sri Lankan Dessert, Watalappan

If you can't have a meal without finishing with something sweet, you need to know about a traditional local dessert called watalappan. On the surface of things, this might seem like a simple custard, but actually the flavour profile is very impressive indeed. The custard contains a mix of coconut milk, jaggery, cashew nuts, eggs, and spices that include cloves, cinnamon, and nutmeg.

92. Feel Calm at the Japanese Peace Pagoda in Galle

If you feel in need of a little peace on your journey, be sure to make your way to the Japanese Peace Pagoda, which you can find on the outskirts of Galle by Unawatuna beach. Peace pagodas around the world were constructed after the Second World War as a way to promote global peace and harmony. There is a staircase to the top of this particular stupa, from which you can take in magnificent views of the ocean.

93. Have a Canyoning Adventure on the River Kelani

If you fancy yourself as something of a thrill seeker, it doesn't get much more adventurous than plunging into a thrashing river and allowing yourself to be carried downwards at full speed. This is known as canyoning, and somewhere to try this out in Sri Lanka is on the Kelani river. There's a few local tour companies that offer this in tandem with kayaking, making for a day in Sri Lanka you're not likely to forget in a hurry.

94. Go Cricket Crazy at the Cricket Club Café

Sri Lanka is a country that is absolutely crazy about the beautiful game of cricket. While you're in the country, it's a good idea to watch a live match, but somewhere else that you can absorb all of the cultural influence that cricket plays in Sri Lanka is at the Cricket Club Café in Colombo. This bungalow café has a beautiful garden and veranda where you can sip on Ceylon tea, and there are always cricket matches being played on the screens.

(34 Queen's Rd, Colombo 00300)

95. Try Deep Sea Fishing Off the Coast of Negombo

If your idea of the perfect getaway involves putting a fishing rod into local waters, why not take your fishing to the next level and try a deep sea fishing experience in Sri Lanka? Negombo on the west coast is the ideal place for this. There are companies that can take you out on to these choppy waters for a fishing experience to remember. Some of the fish in these waters include barracuda, tuna, jackfish, and swordfish, as well as many others.

96. Get to Grips With the Kataragama Esala Festival

The Kataragama temple is a special place in Sri Lanka because it's one of few places that is venerated by Buddhists, Hindus, Moors, and the Vedda People. This means that when the Kataragama Esala festival rolls around, which celebrates the full moon in either late July or early August, it's a time of incredible celebration among the local people. You can see dancing, elephant parades, and if you are lucky, you might even see people walking across burning coals.

97. Be Wowed by the Diyaluma Falls

Something that appeals to everyone, no matter their age or their interests, is a flowing waterfall, and there are plenty of waterfalls to visit in Sri Lanka. One of the very best is Diyulama Falls, which is the second highest waterfall in the country. The falls leap over a dramatic vertical cliff face, which is something breath taking to see up close and in person.

(Colombo - Batticaloa Hwy, Koslanda)

98. Walk Through the Aisles of the Dutch Period Museum

The Dutch ruled the coastal areas of Sri Lanka in parts of the 16th and 17th centuries, and throughout this time they exerted quite an influence on the nation, which was then known as Ceylon. If you would like to know more about this fascinating time in the country's history, the Dutch Period Museum is the ultimate place for a spot of learning. Located inside a 7th century Dutch governor's house, you'll find more than 3000 objects inside.

(Prince Street, Colombo 01100)

99. Take in the Views From Lipton's Seat

Located at the southern edge of the hill country, Haputale is a place of immense natural beauty, and a place that Sir Thomas Lipton, the famous tea baron of Lipton's teas used to enjoy. You'll find this lookout point very close to the Dambatenne tea factory, and it's a wonderful and free spot to survey the natural beauty of the surrounding area, and in the daytime you can also see the tea pickers hard at work.

100. Sip on Decadent Cocktails at Amangalla in Galle

When it gets to Friday night and you've spent the whole week on your feet sightseeing, all you'll want to do is relax in a comfortable environment and sip on a decadent cocktail or two. And this is where Amangalla in Galle comes in. The red tiles rooftop offers the most spectacular sunset views over this charming city, and the cocktails set things off perfectly. The mint julep is a perfect refresher on a balmy evening.

(10 Church St, Galle 80000,
www.aman.com/resorts/amangalla*)*

101. Enjoy the Scenic Journey From Kandy to Ella

The train system in Sri Lanka is not just something functional that allows you to get from A to B. Actually, there are so many scenic rides along this country that the Sri Lankan railways can be seen as an attraction themselves. One of the most beautiful rides has to be from Kandy to Ella and vice versa. On your journey, you'll see carpets of tea bushes, rolling mountains, and local day to day life.

Before You Go...

Thanks for reading **101 Amazing Things to Do in Sri Lanka.** We hope that it makes your trip a memorable one!

Have a great trip!

Team 101 Amazing Things

Manufactured by Amazon.ca
Bolton, ON